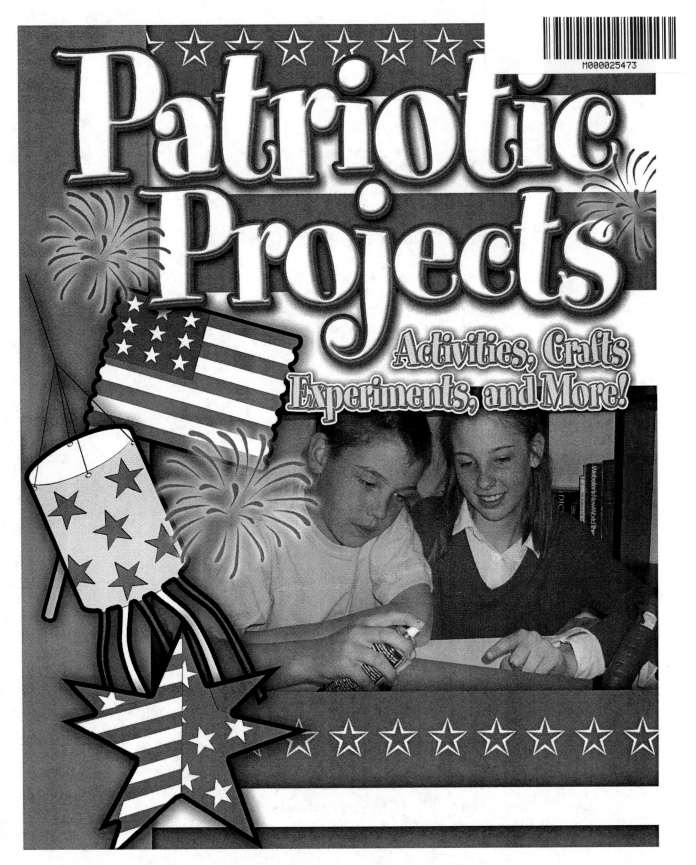

Patriotic Projects

Activities, Crafts Experiments, and More!

Editorial Assistant: Jenny Corsey • Cover Design: Victoria DeJoy
Graphic Design & Layout: Cecil Anderson and Lynette Rowe
Project Illustrations: Michael Dyson

Patriotic Favorites™
Hip! Hip! Hooray! For the U.S.A!

Published by

**GALLOPADE™
INTERNATIONAL**

800-536-2GET
www.gallopade.com

Gallopade is proud to be a member of these educational organizations and associations:

**The National School Supply and Equipment Association (NSSEA)
American Booksellers Association (ABA)
Virginia Educational Media Association (VEMA)
Association of Partners for Public Lands (APPL)
Museum Store Association (MSA)
National Association for Gifted Children (NAGC)
Publishers Marketing Association (PMA)
International Reading Association (IRA)
Association of African American Museums (AAAM)**

Other Patriotic Books

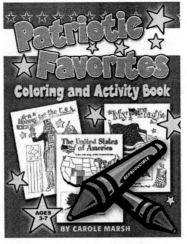

Readers™ about American Patriots
with many more to choose from!

A Word From the Author

Dear Kids,

America is a very special country! This Patriotic Project Book will help you learn more about the United States by completing fun and challenging projects! These stand-alone projects are adaptable for all school ages!

Each project requires everyday materials and natural kid skills like creativity and pizzazz! Hands-on projects help you learn to solve problems and dream up unique solutions. You'll build your research and investigative skills as you search out facts about the United States. Use your skills to have fun learning about our great country and to prepare for your exciting future!

Remember that patriotism is part of what makes America great! Enjoy your Patriotic Project Book experience. It's the trip of a lifetime!

Carole Marsh

Let's get started on this
GREAT PATRIOTIC EXPERIENCE!

Patriotic Windsock

Supplies:

- cylindrical oatmeal box
- blue and white construction paper
- red & white crepe paper streamers
- white yarn or ribbon (strong)
- glue, stapler, scissors, hole punch

Directions:

1. Use scissors to cut off the bottom of the cylindrical box.

2. Glue blue construction paper all over the windsock. Then glue white construction paper stars on the blue.

3. Cut equal sections of red and white crepe paper streamers. Staple them to one end of the windsock.

4. Punch four holes along the top of the windsock. Cut two 12" lengths of yarn or ribbon. Tie the opposite ends of pieces of yarn to the holes on the opposite sides.

5. Tie a longer piece of yarn to the smaller pieces.

6. Hang your patriotic windsock from your window or porch by the longer piece of yarn!

Hang your windsock outside for everyone to see!

Cut off bottom of cylindrical box.

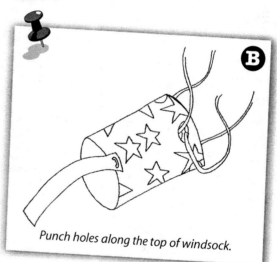

Punch holes along the top of windsock.

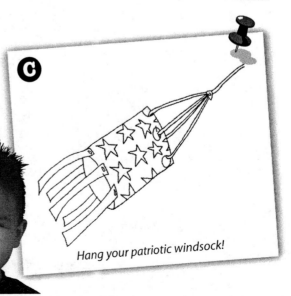

Hang your patriotic windsock!

Icon Match Game

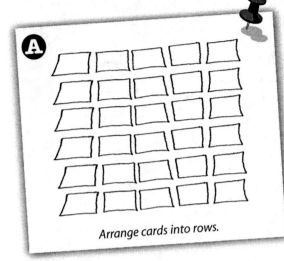

A

Arrange cards into rows.

B

Glue

Glue icons onto each index card.

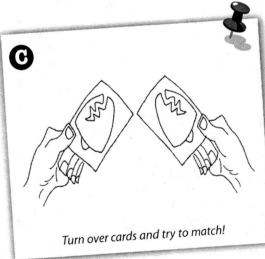

C

Turn over cards and try to match!

Supplies:

- 15 small index cards
- markers or crayons, glue or tape
- chalk, white gel pen, or star stickers
- scissors, black permanent pen
- construction paper or magazine pictures

Directions:

1 Cut each index card in half to make 30 cards. Arrange the cards into a square on the floor (five cards across and six cards down).

2 Color the six upper left cards (two cards across and three cards down) dark blue. Add white stars using chalk, a white gel pen, or star stickers. Color the other cards red and white striped.

3 Use the colored construction paper or magazine pictures to create 15 pairs of American icons (i.e. liberty bell, bald eagle, flag, presidents).

4 Glue icons onto each index card.

5 Turn the cards over and play the matching game with a friend. Each player takes a turn to choose two cards and try making a match. The player with the most matches wins!

TIP: Ask an adult to laminate the cards so they will last longer! Store the cards in a plastic bag for future games.

Stick Flag

Supplies:

- nine craft sticks, glue, scissors
- red & white acrylic paint and brushes
- newspaper sheet
- blue construction paper
- white gel pen

Directions:

Paint craft sticks.

1. Paint five craft sticks red and four craft sticks white.

2. Lay one unpainted whole craft stick down on a sheet of newspaper. Cut or break two other unpainted craft sticks so that only 2/3 remains. Lay them next to the whole stick.

Assemble craft sticks.

3. Glue the painted craft sticks in an alternating pattern to the three unpainted sticks (the base) gluing them across the whole craft sticks.

4. Cut out a small square of bright blue construction paper. Draw white stars on the blue paper with a white gel pen.

5. Glue blue paper square on the flag. Glue another craft stick to the long craft stick on the back.

Salute the flag!

6. Use your little flag to celebrate patriotic holidays!

Presidential Poster

A

Research a president.

B

Mount presidential portrait.

C

Arrange fact cards and display!

Supplies:

- poster board, plain paper
- colored cardboard index cards
- scissors, markers, glue
- gold glitter

Directions:

1 Select your favorite president in U.S. history. Research the life of this president. Write down interesting facts and accomplishments on different colored index cards.

2 Draw pictures of major events in your president's life and time in office and cut them out. Paint a portrait of this president on a large piece of white paper. Cut out a fancy cardboard frame, drizzle glue all over it, and cover it with gold glitter.

3 Write the president's name in glue across the top of a large piece of colorful posterboard. Cover the glue with glitter.

4 Mount your portrait in the middle of the board. Arrange your fact cards and other pictures around the board in chronological order or randomly.

5 Hang your awesome presidential poster in your room!

4th of July Noisemaker

Supplies:

- two pie tins
- dried beans
- red, white, and blue crepe paper
- stapler, gluestick

Directions:

1. Cut six equal strips of crepe paper. Lay the one edge of the strips in the pie pan and glue securely.

2. Pour half a cup of dried beans in the pie tin.

3. Place another pie tin on top and staple all around the edges. Make several noisemakers to share with your friends on the Fourth of July!

A

Glue strips to pie pan.

B

Add in dried beans.

Gather your friends together and have a flag parade.

C

Attach top and make noise!

Strand of Stars

A

Star template.

Supplies:

- red, white, or blue yarn (or string)
- red, white, & blue construction paper
- stapler, scissors, crayons
- tape, or glue, silver glitter

Directions:

1 Decide where you might want to hang your strand of stars. Measure the length of the space and cut as much yarn as you need.

2 Use the star template provided to cut out several red, white, and blue stars from the construction paper. Decorate each star. You can use glitter, construction paper, crayons, buttons, pipe cleaners, anything! Another idea is to paste or draw a picture of a "patriotic face" in the middle of each star.

B

Decorate stars.

3 Arrange the stars in a pattern or any old jumbly way. Fold over one tip of each star over the yarn. Staple, tape, or glue the star tips to the yarn.

4 Leave some yarn on each end to hang the strand of stars. Hang some electric white lights behind the stars to make them glow!

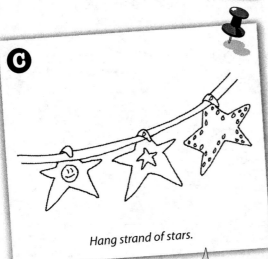

C

Hang strand of stars.

Remember!—a patriot is anyone who loves and serves his or her country, from the U.S. Capitol to your school.

American Door Hanger

A

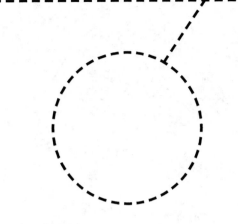

Supplies:

- foam board, poster board, or cardboard
- piece of notebook paper
- patriotic colored construction paper
- scissors, tape or glue

Directions:

1 Trace the template provided on a piece of notebook paper. Use the template to cut out a door hanger from either foam board, poster board, or cardboard. Be sure to cut out the circle in the middle so it will fit on a door!

2 Cover the door hanger with patriotic construction paper using tape or glue. Be creative! Cut out stars, color pictures, make a flag, write U.S.A. in glitter at the bottom, anything to make your door hanger look patriotic.

3 Let the door hanger dry if needed. Hang your patriotic creation on your door to let everyone know that you're an American patriot!

TIP: Poke a pencil through the top circle in the door hanger. Then cut the circle from the inside out!

Patriotic Poet

Read "The Star-Spangled Banner" aloud.

Write a patriotic poem.

Supplies:

- creativity and imagination
- dictionary and thesaurus
- sharp pencils, paper
- inexpensive picture frame

Directions:

1. Francis Scott Key's famous poem, The Star-Spangled Banner, inspired our national anthem. Read the poem aloud.

2. Use your imagination to write a poem that you think could inspire people to become more patriotic, more loyal, and more devoted to the United States.

3. Ask an adult to proofread your poem. Then copy the final version onto a clean piece of paper and frame it. Hang the poem in your room!

Display your patriotic poem!

Fast Fact! Fast Fact! In 1905, Sharlot Hall wrote a poem that inspired people to make Arizona a state! She was only twelve years old!

Think about how wonderful it is to be an American. Then write a patriotic poem!

Victory Spirit Rocks

Supplies:

- several clean rocks
- acrylic paints
- creativity and imagination

Directions:

1 Find several smooth, round rocks in different sizes and colors (light or dark). Some of your rocks might be the size of a tennis ball while others could be about the size of a softball or grapefruit.

2 Clean the rocks very well with soap and water. Remove all dirt, weeds, and especially BUGS from the rocks! Let the rocks dry in the sun or on an old towel.

3 Once the rocks are dry, use the paint to decorate them. Make each spirit rock unique. You may want to paint patriotic symbols, write patriotic words, or use patriotic colors.

4 After decorating, let each spirit rock dry for several hours. Assemble the rocks in your yard to make a rock garden. Line them up on your windowsill. Use them as paperweights for your desk. Or give them away to inspire others to be more patriotic!

Find some smooth rocks.

Paint your rocks.

Display your rock garden!

Liberty Pops

Bring mixture to a boil.

Turn sticks to cover in syrup.

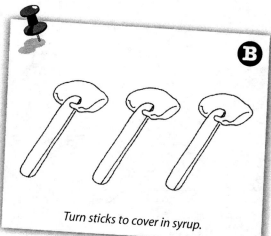

Enjoy your liberty pops!

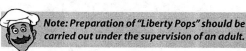
Note: Preparation of "Liberty Pops" should be carried out under the supervision of an adult.

Supplies:

- 1 cup sugar
- 1/2 cup water
- 1/3 cup light corn syrup
- 1/4 cup cranraspberry concentrate
- 24 six-inch lollipop sticks
- vegetable oil
- candy thermometer

Directions:

1. Combine sugar, water, and corn syrup in a small saucepan. Bring mixture to a boil, stirring until sugar dissolves. Then boil on high heat without stirring until the syrup reaches 280°.

2. Add cranraspberry concentrate. Cook mixture on moderately-high heat until syrup reaches 300°. Dip saucepan into one inch of cold water briefly to stop boiling.

3. Spoon 6 small tablespoons of syrup into circles about two inches apart onto oiled baking sheets.

4. Quickly place a stick into each lollipop. Turn each stick to cover with syrup so they will stick well. Continue, 6 at a time.

5. When the lollipops harden, enjoy! (Wrap extras in plastic wrap.)

Patriotic Pencil Holder

Supplies:

- 15 craft sticks (Popsicle sticks)
- newspaper sheets, cardboard
- acrylic paints and paintbrush
- empty toilet paper holder
- tacky glue, rubber bands

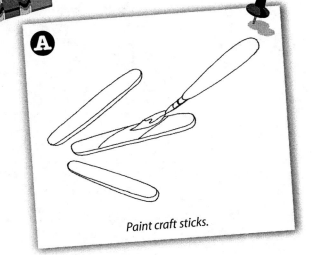

Paint craft sticks.

Directions:

1 Paint the craft sticks in patriotic colors. You can paint each one a solid color or use several colors for each one. Let each one dry on newspaper so paint won't get everywhere.

2 Make a cardboard circle by tracing one end of the paper holder. Cut out the circle. Glue it to one end of the paper holder and let it dry.

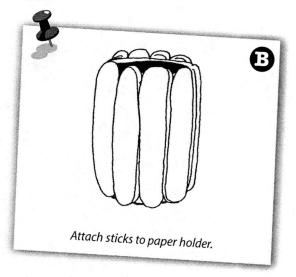

Attach sticks to paper holder.

3 Cover the paper holder with one light coat of tacky glue. Attach the painted sticks to cover the tube. They should line up tightly side by side. Wrap the holder with rubber bands to secure the sticks until the glue dries.

4 Decorate with stickers, glitter, or other patriotic objects if you wish. Fill the holder with red, white, and blue pencils and set it on your desk!

Decorate and enjoy!

Uncle Sam Clothespin

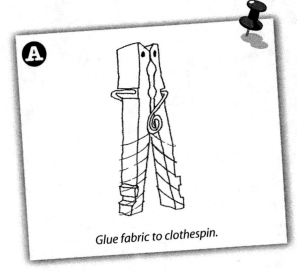

Glue fabric to clothespin.

Supplies:

- old-fashioned wooden clothespin
- fabric scissors
- fabric with patriotic designs & colors
- wooden skewers
- glue, black ink pen, cardboard, cotton ball, blue & red felt-tipped pens
- small rectangular piece of white paper and toothpick

Glue cotton and hat to clothespin.

Directions:

1. Cut fabric for Uncle Sam's shirt and pants. Glue them securely. Wrap the pants around the forks.

2. Wrap the shirt fabric around two small equal lengths of a skewer to make arms. Glue them to the clothespin.

3. Glue cotton to give Uncle Sam hair and a fluffy beard. Make eyes with a felt-tipped pen.

4. Make the hat's brim by covering a tiny cardboard circle with fabric. Roll up a strip of paper, cover it with fabric for the top of the hat, and attach it to the brim. Secure the hat to Uncle Sam's head.

5. Make a flag with the pens and white paper. Then glue it to a toothpick. Attach the flag to one of Uncle Sam's arms.

Attach flag to Uncle Sam's arm.

Independence Day Puzzle

Supplies:

- 8 empty, clean small juice boxes
- gluestick, scissors, pencil
- patriotic picture from magazine, coloring book page, or colored markers and white paper

Arrange juice boxes.

Directions:

1. Lay out the juice boxes in two rows of four. Your rectangle should measure about seven inches by seven inches. Choose a patriotic picture from a magazine, a completed coloring book page, or draw your own picture.

2. Lay the picture faced down. Arrange the rectangle of boxes on top. Trace around the boxes with a pencil to make a grid of eight rectangles on the paper. Cut the outlined picture into the eight pieces.

Cut the picture into juice-box shapes.

3. Turn the pieces over and reassemble them to look like the original picture. Lay them on the juice box rectangle. Glue each picture piece to its corresponding box. Let them dry.

4. Mix up the picture boxes and see how fast you can put it back together!

For a greater challenge, cover the front and back of each box with a different picture.

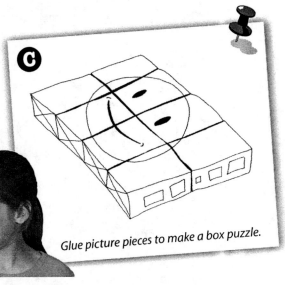

Glue picture pieces to make a box puzzle.

Fireworks Painter's Cap

A

Draw stars on painter's cap.

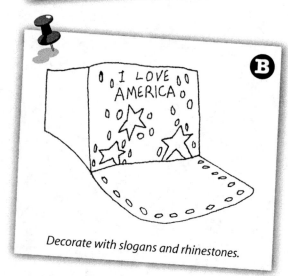

B

Decorate with slogans and rhinestones.

C

Wear your cap!

Supplies:

- plain white painter's cap
- red, white, blue, and green fabric
- markers, craft glue
- multi-colored rhinestones (buy at any craft store)

Directions:

1. Use fabric markers in every color to draw huge starbursts on the front part of the cap. Give them trailers so they look like real fireworks.

2. Draw smaller colored starbursts on the front bill. Then write a patriotic saying using different colors for each word. Some examples of sayings are: "God bless America," "Land of the Free," "I love America," "Freedom Forever," and "U.S.A."

3. Glue different colored rhinestones in the center of each starburst and on each tip. Let them dry. Then wear your cap in the sun so everyone can watch you sparkle!

Remember!—only use fireworks under adult supervision!

Fireworks Art

Wear your Fireworks Painter's Cap and let's get started!

A

Glue and glitter great designs.

GLITTER

Use glue to make designs on a large piece of black construction paper. Sprinkle colored glitter on next. Let dry, then slide excess glitter off the picture.

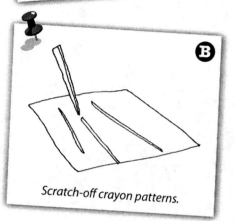

B

Scratch-off crayon patterns.

CRAYON

Color a piece of paper with crayons. Cover the entire paper. Paint over with ink or black poster paint. When it dries, scratch off fireworks designs in the "night sky" with a toothpick.

C

Paint a fireworks frenzy!

PAINT

Do this project outdoors! Use a small paintbrush to splatter colored paints on black construction paper. Drop 8" lengths of yarn in the paint. Then drag it on the paper to create several lines that stream out from each burst like fireworks.

D

Colorful candy makes a splash!

CANDY

Dip sponges into colored tempera paints. Dab them on a piece of black construction paper to create fireworks bursts. Glue several brightly colored candy pieces in patterns on the bursts to add a three-dimensional look to the fireworks.

Lincoln's Log Cabin

Cover carton with peanut butter.

Supplies:

- 12" x 18" piece of cardboard
- small milk carton
- creamy peanut butter
- chocolate-covered raisins
- pretzel sticks
- graham crackers
- slivered almonds
- 8 oz. white frosting
- bag of coconut flakes
- green food coloring

Stick food onto peanut butter.

Directions:

1. Cover the cardboard with foil, securing it with tape. Cut off bottom of the milk carton. Tape to the cardboard.

2. Cover the carton with peanut butter. Use graham crackers for windows, a roof, and a door. Use pretzel-stick "logs" to finish the rest.

3. Paste three rows of the chocolate-covered raisins along the sides and back of the house to make a "stone" foundation. Spread peanut butter and lay rows of slivered almonds to make a path.

4. Mix 8 ounces of white frosting, 8 drops of green food coloring, and half a cup of coconut flakes in a small bowl. Spread green frosting "grass" around the log cabin.

Make frosting and coconut "grass."

Patriotic Paperweights

Supplies:

- plaster of Paris, waxed paper
- plastic knife, disposable bowl
- permanent marker, scissors
- star-shaped cookie cutter
- clear craft glue
- glitter (silver, red, and blue)
- plastic gems, beads, tiny buttons, wire coils, etc. in silver, red, and blue

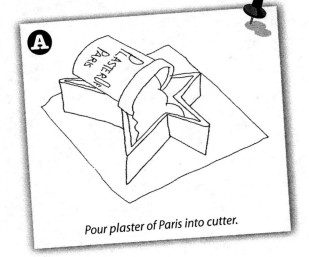

Pour plaster of Paris into cutter.

Directions:

1. Trace around the cookie cutter on a piece of waxed paper. Then cut out a star shape that is 1/2" beyond your outline. Press the wax paper shape into the cookie cutter. It should be big enough to fold up along the sides.

2. Pour the plaster of Paris into the waxed-paper-lined star shape. Fill it 3/4 full. Smooth the surface with a plastic knife.

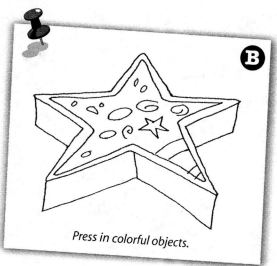

Press in colorful objects.

3. Quickly press the objects into wet plaster where you think they look best. Let the plaster dry completely.

4. Remove the plaster star from the cookie cutter by lifting out the waxed paper. Spread a light coat of glue on the outside of the plaster star shape. Sprinkle glitter on the wet glue.

Use your patriotic paper weight.

Uncle Sam's Tall Hat

Supplies:

- One 24" x 35" sheet each of red, white, and blue poster board
- glue, cellophane tape, pencil, ruler
- measuring tape, scissors
- buttons (all colors)

Directions:

1. Cut a large circle (16" diameter) from the blue poster board.

2. Now find the circumference of your head by wrapping a measuring tape around your head, and add 1" to this number.

3. Cut a piece of red poster board that is 12" tall and your head-circumference wide. Roll the poster board into a tube and tape the ends.

4. Fold flaps toward the center of the tube and tape securely. Cut a circle of red poster board and glue it onto the top.

5. On the bottom end of the red tube, cut vertical slits 2" inches apart all the way around. Tape the cut sections under the brim to attach the pieces together.

6. Glue 2" white strips on the red poster board every 2". Cut a two-inch blue strip and glue it around the bottom of the tube for a hatband.

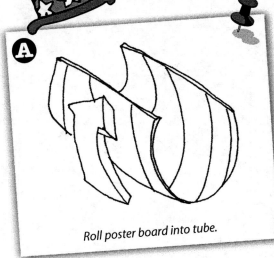

A

Roll poster board into tube.

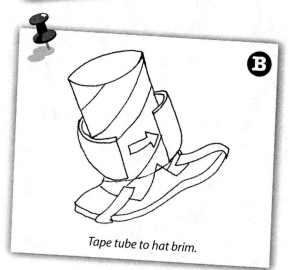

B

Tape tube to hat brim.

C

Glue on strip and hat band.

Fourth of July Collage

Supplies:

- piece of white or colored poster board
- old magazines, catalogs, etc.
- glue sticks or tacky glue and scissors

Directions:

1. Browse through the magazines, catalogs, newspapers, postcards, and whatever else you can find. Look for pictures that represent America, freedom, independence, and patriotism. Cut out several pictures until you have a decent sized pile.

2. First spread out all the pictures on the poster board. See what looks best together. How can you arrange it differently?

3. When you have decided where the pictures should go, glue each one to the poster board. It's okay if some parts overlap. Add red, white, and blue ribbons or streamers to the outside to give your collage a patriotic border. Hang the collage in your room!

TIP: Don't use too much glue. A light coat is more than enough. Too much glue will make the picture look wet, then wrinkled when it dries.

Cut out patriotic pictures.

Arrange pictures on poster board.

Glue pictures on poster board.

Liberty Bell Craft

Cover cup with aluminum.

Attach bell to cup.

Let freedom ring!

Supplies:

- paper or Styrofoam cup
- pencil, tape, aluminum foil
- 2 pipe cleaners (white, red, or blue)
- small jingle bell and star stickers

Directions:

1. Poke a tiny hole in the middle of the bottom of the cup with a pencil. Cut a piece of aluminum foil big enough to cover the cup and hang over the top and bottom about an inch. Cover the cup and tape the foil in place (glue won't work). Fold the extra foil neatly inside and tape securely.

2. String the jingle bell into the middle of a pipe cleaner. Fold in half. Insert both ends through the tiny hole in the cup. Pull them through until the bell hangs about an inch from the top edge of the cup's inside.

3. Fold the other pipe cleaner in half for a hanger. Twist the two ends of this pipe cleaner with the two ends of the other one to attach them. Flatten the wrapped sections down on the bottom of the cup as much as possible and tape securely. Cover this by folding down the extra foil and taping in place.

TIP: You could also add more foil to create a flared look for the bottom of the bell!

Fun Flag Cake

Supplies:

- 1 box of cake mix (any flavor)
- can of white frosting
- several bags of candy pieces
- several packs of lifesavers
- large bag of gumdrops
- large bag of red-hot candies

Directions:

1 Bake cake according to instructions on the box. Let it cool. Frost cake with a thick layer of white frosting. Decorate the top of the cake to look like a flag. There should be a square in the upper left for the blue stars, seven red stripes, and six white stripes.

2 For red stripes, use red-hot candies, other red candy, strawberries, or raspberries.

3 For white stripes, use white chocolate pieces or shredded coconut.

4 Fill the blue section or make blue stars with blue candies, blueberries, or blue jellybeans. If you fill the blue section, make white stars on top of the blue section with frosting.

TIP: You can also use red and white sprinkles in rows to make stripes.

A Frost the top of baked cake.

B Decorate with favorite flag food.

C Have your cake and eat it, too!

Note: Preparation of the "Fun Flag Cake" should be carried out under adult supervision.

Presidential Pins

Glue cardboard strip to lids.

Attach felt to lids.

Draw faces and display!

Supplies:

- two large plastic juice bottle caps
- craft glue
- 1 - sheet each of black, gray, peach, and white felt
- 1 inch wide pin back

Directions:

1. Glue a short cardboard strip across the back of each juice bottle lid. Then glue the pin back on each.

2. Trace a lid on the peach felt. Cut two peach circles and glue one on the top of each lid.

3. Draw some patriotic designs on plain paper to use as a pattern. Use pictures of patriotic symbols for the pattern. Cut out the pattern.

4. Trace the patterns on felt using permanent marker. Cut out the pattern from the felt and glue onto the presidential pins.

5. Use a permanent marker to draw a face or add color to the presidential pin.

You and your friends could start pin collections and trade them!

Patriotic Pinwheel

Supplies:

- 2 pieces of thick construction
- paper or heavy card stock
- scissors, hole punch, markers, crayons
- push pin or tack
- unsharpened pencil with eraser
- patriotic stickers

Directions:

1 Fold the corners of both sheets down to make two squares and cut off the top rectangle. Fold the squares in half to make two triangles. Then fold them again so that each square has an "x" crease in the middle when unfolded.

2 Decorate one side of each paper square with colored markers, crayons, and patriotic stickers.

3 Hold the undecorated sides of both papers together with paper clips on all four sides. Make four cuts along the creased fold lines, halfway to the center of the squares.

4 Punch a hole in each corner of the squares. Fold each corner with a hole to the center. Push the tack through the four punched holes and through the center of the pinwheel. Then push the pin into the pencil eraser to attach the pinwheel.

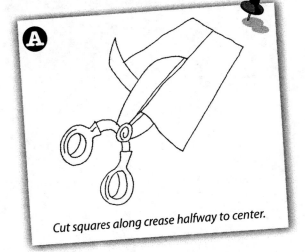

A Cut squares along crease halfway to center.

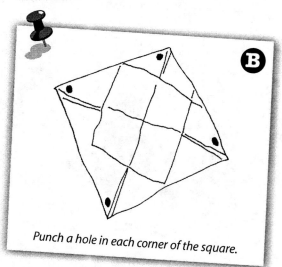

B Punch a hole in each corner of the square.

C Attach pinwheel to pencil!

Bald Eagle Puppet

Glue head over the top of paper bag.

Attach wings to inside-fold of bag.

Attach tail feathers and fly away!

Supplies:

- lunch-size brown paper bag
- colored markers or crayons or paints
- black, yellow, and white construction paper
- gluestick, scissors

Directions:

1. Lay the paper bag flat—fold on top. Cut an eagle-shaped head from white construction paper. Color the edges black. Glue the head over the top, not below the flap.

2. Cut a curved beak shape from yellow construction paper. Cut two circles from black construction paper. Glue the beak and eyes on the eagle head.

3. Cut a rectangle from black construction paper to fit the front of the paper bag. Glue it under the flap.

4. Cut out a right and left wing from black construction paper. Make them as big as you like. Glue the tips of the wings on the upper sides of the flattened paper bag, inside the folds.

5. Cut out either a tail flap or several tail feathers from white construction paper. Glue these just under the top section of the paper bag at the bottom. Cut out and glue on yellow talons and white tail feathers.

Patriotic Magnet Frame

Supplies:

- Two 5" x 7" frames cut from heavy-duty magnetic sheeting
- 5" x 7" piece of cardboard
- red and blue vinyl tape
- 5" x 7" piece of white paper
- white star stickers

Directions:

1. Glue the cardboard onto one of the magnets. Glue the piece of white paper onto the cardboard.

2. Lay long strips of red tape, alternating with white spaces for stripes, on the magnet. Press firmly until they stick.

3. Lay short strips of blue vinyl tape in the upper left corner of the frame to create a square. Use white star stickers on the blue square.

4. Cut a square or oval opening for the picture to show through.

5. Attach a photograph to the second magnet by placing a dot of glue in each corner.

6. Glue the decorated flag magnet on top of the photographed magnet so that the picture shows through the opening.

A

Create a decorative frame.

B

Attach a picture to second magnet.

C

Glue the two magnets together!

President's Day Wind Chime

Make holes in bottom of coffee can.

Stripe can with ribbons.

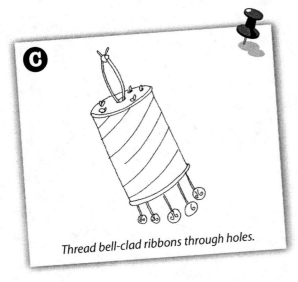
Thread bell-clad ribbons through holes.

Supplies:

- craft glue
- hammer & nail and metal coffee can
- 2" wide ribbon (red, white, & blue)
- 3" wide patterned ribbon (patriotic design)
  narrow ribbon (red, white, & blue)
- 6-8 small gold tone bells
- 6-8 small silver tone star-shaped bells

Directions:

1. Use the hammer and nail to drive one hole in the center of the bottom. Then make 15 more holes evenly spaced around the center.

2. Use glue and the 3" wide patterned ribbon to completely cover the outside of the canister. Use the 2" wide ribbon creatively to decorate with stripes.

3. Use a thicker, sturdier ribbon for the center hole. Loop and knot it to hang the wind chime on a hook or tree branch outside.

4. Cut the narrow ribbon in lengths about twice as long as the canister, some longer and some shorter (five of each color). Thread the narrow ribbons through the holes and tie large knots at the top so they cannot slip through the bottom of the canister. Tie bells on the ends of the ribbons.

Patriot's Pen

Supplies:

- hole-punch, gluestick
- red and blue construction paper (one piece of each color)
- plain white stationary
- red or blue gel pen
- sheet of notebook paper

Directions:

Write a letter to a soldier or sailor.

1. Write a letter to a soldier or sailor on a sheet of paper. Ask questions about his or her job, duties, and background. Tell this person why you are writing a letter, why you are a patriot, and why you love your country. Ask for a letter in return!

Create a patriotic border.

2. Use the hole punch and construction paper to create a small pile of tiny red and blue circles. Glue the dots in fancy designs around the border of the letter and on the outside of the envelope.

3. You may want to tuck a recent school photo in the envelope, so your soldier or sailor will know who is sending this letter!

Mail your message to a patriotic pen-pal!

4. Ask an adult to help you mail the letter!

Buy a patriotic stamp at your local post office to put on your letter!

Standing Star

A

Star template.

Supplies:

- stiff paper (card stock, oaktag, or thin cardboard)
- scissors, tape
- crayons, markers, glitter, glue, etc.

Directions:

1. Use the pattern to cut out two identical stars from your stiff paper.

2. Decorate each star on both sides with crayons, markers, glitter, and other colorful craft supplies. One could be colored with red and white stripes, and the other could be colored blue with white or glittery stars.

3. Make one slit in each star. Cut a slit from an inner corner to the center point of the first star. Cut a slit on the second star from an outer corner to the center point.

4. Slide the two stars together through the slits that were cut. Use tape where the stars meet at the slits for added stability.

5. Set your freestanding three-dimensional star decoration on your desk or kitchen table!

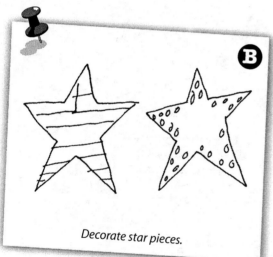

B

Decorate star pieces.

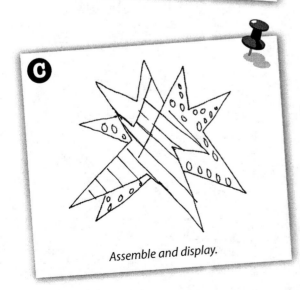

C

Assemble and display.